HIS THOUGHTS CONCERN ME

HIS THOUGHTS CONCERN ME

C.H. CHRISTOPHER

To order additional copies of this book, contact:
Xlibris
1-888-795-4274
www.Xlibris.com
Orders@Xlibris.com
754776

TABLE OF CONTENTS

CHAPTER 1

HUMBLE BEGINNINGS

I was born in Milwaukee, Wisconsin, on April 20, 1953, to Florence Leticia Dawson and Archie Dawson, a resident of Chicago. I had three older sisters. The next year my brother, Vincent Arturo was born. In fact he and I were eleven months apart, that meant that every year for one month we were the same age. We found that amusing. Honestly, we found nearly everything about life amusing. Mom would try to our silliness under control but her efforts were futile. I believe we had cartoon minds back then. We had to find fun and laughter in everything. We loved to play and read and laugh all the time. I thought we really had a funny bone in us. Mom had to separate at times so we could be quiet. We weren't mean just silly. When we went to the library every Saturday, we would be quiet just long enough to find a Dr. Suess book so we could laugh some more. We really loved reading books. Once we pretended we were sick in order to stay home from school to read Dr. Seuss' "Sleep Book." We even got to stay in mom's bed. We snook the book under the covers and waited our opportunity. Mom had made us fresh squeezed orange juice and went to her office. We thought we were safe but a half hour later we voices. It was a family friend. The prayingest man we ever heard! Mom thought we needed his prayers! We pulled the covers over our heads and stayed until was through. It seemed like a hour, and he prayed for us and it seemed our future families! I was scared and so was Vince. We decided we were well enough to go to school the next day! Secretly I always felt that mom knew...That didn't keep us from further foolishness either.

Every April Fool's Day was an invitation to mischief for my brother and I. One April Fool's day we planned to punk our neighbor. He would come over every Saturday morning and get a bowl of

Cornflakes. Our door was never locked and only my dad would be up working in his garden. Vince and I came up with the idea of changing the sugar in the sugar bowl to salt, just to see the look on our neighbor's face. Our friend and his family had been our friends for a longtime, so he was welcome. Vincent and I hid in the kitchen cabinet to watch Sure enough, like usual this neighbor came in, got a bowl, poured some Cornflakes. He took a tablespoon and sprinkled onto the flakes. He took the milk and poured some on. Sitting at the big kitchen table he took a spoonful. His face turned red, I never saw anything like it. He dumped out the cereal and ran out the kitchen door. Vince and I roared with laughter til dad came in. Again we hid.

Dad poured his morning Butternut brand coffee. He reached for the creamer then the sugar. Vince let out a giggle. I covered his mouth. When dad put the cup to his lips, I couldn't keep from laughing. Dad simply got up from the table took off his belt, opened the cabinet and we tumbled out ; while he gave us a what we deserved! We really got a good one. We never did that again.

Foolishness is bound in the heart of a child…My mom loved to entertain guests and make beautiful meals in the dining room. It seated twelve and we also had a children's table. You had to earn the right to sit at the big dining table. Our regular daily meals were served at the large kitchen which also seated twelve Mom had complete tablescapes with table cloth, napkins, doilies, matching silverware, and cups for every meal. You were expected to use table manners at all times. We were taught proper dining etiquette very early in life.

When adults were talking you said nothing. You asked for items to be passed to you, by saying please and thank you. Evening meals were served with hot tea as beverage.

One afternoon my brother and I watched "The Howdy Doody" show on television then we heard it's time for dinner. We washed our hands and sat at the table. Vincent being the youngest at the time, was seated right next mom. I was seated directly across from mom, with dad at the bead of the table. Dinner was great Then we had tea when mom was pouring around the table, Vincent began making faces like Howdy Doody. I just looked away to keep from laughing. Then mom sat back down. Vincent made a face just as I took a gulp of warm tea which made me spray across the table on mom, she was outraged! She made me and Vincent go to bed early without getting any dessert, which happened to be my favorite double chocolate layer cake. We knew our shenanigans were costing us too much, but couldn't resist silliness.

Getting older and maturing helped both of us immensely. I was delightful in school, smart and well liked. My teachers would say the same thing on every grade school report card. I thought there was a problem, so I asked my mom what they meant by "a well adjusted child?" Since every teacher from kindergarten through sixth grade wrote the same thing in the comments on all my report cards. Mom explained that it meant I was able to accept the rules and follow directions and cooperate. I was okay with it, then.

I didn't want to be bullied and wouldn't fight unless provoked to. I was known to be part of the pretty girl club, so all the "tomboys" would threaten to scratch up my face. I didn't understand people like that, and spent many hours trying to figure them out, until I had the revelation that some people don't want to be happy, and want you to be miserable, too. The problem was that I had a sunny disposition. I couldn't wait for another sunrise to see what a day would bring. I was thankful for whatever went on today, but look forward to the future with hope and anticipation. I used to love to meet new people, because I felt that they should meet me. And most people were.

While I was seemingly easy prey for bullies, God protected me from hurt and harm. I never had fight and never got bloodied by the bullies that went to our public school. Got threatened with bodily harm several times, but I would just stare at the perp, and they thought there was something supernatural or other worldly going on.

Something was keeping them from hitting me. It was angels guarding me, even when I didn't know God. My mom prayed for us all the time. I felt a protection around me nearly all the time. Praise God for a praying mom.

CHAPTER 2

WRONG PATH

My life took a deep turn when I graduated from High School. Having gone to a private girls' high school made me appreciate boys in a different way. I had three great protective brothers, but was naive about men. My junior year, I was working for the City. I met a lady that invited me to a family function.

There I met a guy that interested me. We danced and talked for hours and found we had some things in common. Neither of us knew Jesus though. We dated for a year when he asked to date only him. A year after that we moved in together. We were inseparable. Friends began telling me that in order to keep him, I needed to show that I loved him, by being intimate with him. I thought that ridiculous at first and because I wanted to be celebate until I got married. The guy was sending me conflicting signals. Eventually, I caved to the pressure. I felt I had betrayed myself. Long story short, he proved not the one for me. I was always looking for a way out of the relationship. When I came to the Lord, I got the courage to let it go and the relationship was over.

Jesus rescued me from that situation and more. I believed I had lost my way and my joy in that relationship. Sin always causes you to lose your Joy. Lesson learned.

Chapter 3

CHILD PRODIGY AND IMMORTALITY

I remember auditioning often after school when I was in elementary school. Back then agents came to our house and sometimes I didn't know which of us children they were interested in. The only way I could tell was if I was alone with the agent and my parents.

Sometimes mom would have me recite something or dance for them. I thought she was just showing me off at first. Later I was sent to audition at their studio. Mom would take me there, but she didn't go into the room where I would meet several people who asked me to sing, dance, or recite a poem, etc. They started saying I was a child prodigy like Shirley Temple. I knew there was money being paid to mom for my performances, but didn't ask questions.

After a while I felt a bit pressured to perform well instead of enjoying it as in the past.

Once a recording agent came to our house. Me and both my parents met. This time they wanted me to sing. At the time my repertoire including songs like "It's a Most Unusual Day," "Singing In the Rain, "I got Rhythm," mainly songs I heard on television. I saw the agent smiling and told my folks they wanted me to audition for some execs from the company. I had to meet with them at what appeared to be a small hotel room with recording equipment. Two men and a lady met with me. They showed me a contract telling me I was to fly to California and do a screen test, but they wanted me to take the contract, have my parents sign it, and they would begin the process of making me a star. I was excited about it all except the part where I was to go to California! I was to go alone! Not my family! Me alone! When I gave my mom the contract, she was thrilled, but I wasn't! I asked if she or dad could come with me, but the agency was only interested in me. Mom said it was a great opportunity for me, but she understood my hesitance.

It was only a week later that the agency made contact with us about our decision. I could see that Mom was happy for me, but something inside me said don't go, so I told mom I wasn't going to California. She was sad, because we needed the money. I felt that I let the family down. Funny how after all these years, I have not wanted to go there, and haven't ever gone to California.

I realized that God had made me immortal through several experiences. When I was a few days old I began to have breathing problems. Mom says I just stopped breathing. I was put in the iron lung and my mom prayed for me. I came home but had episodes of what appeared to be asthma, even though I was never diagnosed as asthmatic. I was determined to beat it. I prayed to myself because I didn't know God, and said I will not be out of breath when we play games anymore. I didn't want to go in the house because of breathing spells, any more. One night it came to me that I should fill the bathroom face bowl with cold water and put my face in it until the panic came.

At first I could only do it a few seconds. I did this every night for about three weeks and I eventually was able to hold my breath with face in that face bowl without panicking at all. I was free of whatever asthmatic symptoms I had and could run around playing with my friends with no complications.

Next God showed me His immortality when I was invited to sing at a friend's mother's funeral in Chicago one summer. I had tried to witness to this friend but he was not wanting to give up his sinful lifestyle. Again I was praying that I would sing something that could make him change his attitude. I was sitting in funeral parlor when I felt thirsty. I got up to get a drink from the hallway water fountain. I bent down and took a drink but when I stood up I felt faint. The room was spinning. The guy I was with came to see what was taking me so long.

I collapsed in his arms. I could see him but knew I was someplace other than there. I heard these words "Say, Jesus is the Lord and Giver of Life." I felt myself leaving my body, but couldn't help it. I kept hearing, "Say, Jesus is the Lord and Giver of Life." I looked in the face of the one holding me up and he was terrified. He said something but I could not understand. The Lord said, "Now he is holding eternity in his hands." Then I heard, "Say Jesus is the Lord and Giver of Life." I whispered it then I was back. My friend just stood there as if he had seen a ghost. Immediately I was so cold but needed to sing. I sang, "He'll Understand and Say Well done." Afterward I didn't have body heat for two days. Eventually my body felt normal. My friend couldn't wrap his mind around that experience, but God told me to never see him again.

I realized that I am God's property, and as such He can do whatever is in His will for me, without question, doubts, or fears.

CHAPTER 4

SET TO STAND OUT AND EARLY REVELATIONS

Ever since I could remember I loved to sing. If I heard a song anywhere I would sing it until I sounded like whoever sang. When I was in grade school I heard my mom playing the piano and singing a church song every morning and knew the way it made me feel to hear her sweetly singing, "Bless This House." I decided to pray that I could sing too. Mom was a soloist at our historical Church.

I believed mom was valuable to our church and community because dignitaries were always over our house. Sometimes we would have the Governor, Pastors, Aldermen, police officers, choir directors etc., dining with us.

I knew we must have been a special family. My love for singing lead me to go anywhere my mom went to sing or listen to someone else speak or sing. She didn't mind my tagging along because she I had a gift of remembering everything I heard including, piano playing accompaniments and solos. I loved to hear great singing. Mahalia Jackson, Marian Anderson,Dorothy Dandridge, and Leontyne Price filled my musical life.

As I grew, I found myself swept up by the vocal stylings of Dionne Warrick, Barbara Streisand, the Supremes, Petula Clark, and the Carpenters. These artists gave me plenty of material to perfect in my singing repertoire. I remembered in fourth grade singing "To Sir with Love," and the teacher asked me where that voice came from. I didn't know what she meant so I sat down. The word spread that I was singing all the hits like the artist and my friends started sending their friends and family to hear me sing. Of course, I didn't mind a bit, because I wanted to always sing.

I will never forget my Freshman year in High School. They were having a talent show and anyone could be in it. There were only six persons of color in that private school so I was hesitant at first. Even the six of us black girls didn't really know each other but I wanted to share my voice too. So I signed up. I sang from the middle of the gym floor without a mic," Alfie," and the audience erupted with applause and chants of "encore, encore," then someone yelled out "sing something else." I sang Roberta Flack's hit, "Killing Me Softly." I became known as a singer. I became president of our Glee Club. High School proved to be a very rewarding experience to me. I knew it was part of God's plan. My range of music interest was wide from classical to gospel, from pop to Broadway and R&B. I was beginning to get known in live entertainment venues even though I was only 18.

Nightclub owners would let me sing but not drink. One night I got into trouble because I didn't notice a place that had musical guest in the house. I knew the owner and he introduced me and I went and performed the hit, "Yes I'm Ready," to a thunderous applause. The trouble came when they announced their guest, who happened to be the original artist! Ouch! I can't tell you how I felt that night. Anyway I checked next time…

Growing up with four sisters had its perks. I had examples of how to conduct myself and what to wear. I would ask my sisters about things pertaining to relationships, etc. We were pretty much together all the time from fifth grade and up, then some of my sisters went to high school where challenges began.

Generally we weren't allowed to go further than our four square block, and we knew everyone on that block. When I was in sixth grade three new families moved into our block. One particular family moved into a two-flat and we never saw any adults there. There were three elder young men and two younger teen-age boys. We would go past their house and noticed one of the boys was very friendly towards one of my siblings. His friends appeared to be different in an odd way. My mom always met new people who moved in and said that they were grown men and cousins living together in the duplex but they seemed nice. The sibling was dating age and met the boy, our new neighbor at the high school and I could tell she liked him. They walked home together and he came over a couple times to play in our yard. I saw some guys around their house smoking and drinking in the yard from time to time. Once we were talking about our neighbor and his cousins, when I said," I thought they were trouble." Instantly my sister chimed in with, "You don't know what you are talking about." I really didn't. Mom gave me a Be quiet look. I really didn't know why I said it either.

Three days later, I was walking home from school with my brother when I had a vision of police and ambulances on our block sirens blaring. When we got two blocks from home, we see police and emergency vehicles blocking the street in front of what looked like our new neighbors' house. Everyone crowded the street. When I asked," What happened?" My mom said the neighbor and some boys were playing Russian Roulette and the gun went off!" Someone in the house was taken into custody and that ended our relationship with them. I wasn't sure why I knew that.

CHAPTER 5

UNTRAINED CHURCH MUSICIAN

I began piano playing well when I was a child. God gifted me with it and I enjoyed making up songs as well as accompanying others on piano. They called it playing by ear. My mom would send my sister and I to churches that needed a musician, because we could figure out the accompaniment to whatever they were singing. We learned to play for the Pentecostal churches mostly. We just went on and played. They sometimes gave us cookies or koolaid or prayed for us. They would call mom and she would send us on our way.

I appreciated it more when I got older and my husband and I visited a large Baptist church. Sunday School was great. Then the deacons came up to start their devotional. I heard one praying that God would send their church a musician because their organist had just passed away and their pianist was in the hospital. I quietly prayed Lord you can do this. I'm willing, and I sat there. Then I saw the large choir lined up at the center doors. I heard, "Go now." I quietly sat down at the piano. They began to sing one line of "One More Time," and I began to play the song I had never heard before. When Pastor came in he was surprised that God had answered so soon. I was their musician for about four months until the pianist was fully recovered.

Chapter 6

GREAT LEADERS OF MY TIME

I began learning lessons not only in school but amazingly I got some important lessons while attending churches throughout my life. As early as I can remember our family attended St. Matthews CME, Christian Methodist Church. It was a historic church, means really old. Our family apparently had been founders of this Church with several Aunts and Uncles they addressed as "Bishop", and "Reverend." It was a special day whenever they visited our local congregation. I believe that was the main reason we attended St. Matthews. It was at that church where I met the late President John Kennedy, Senator Edward "Ted" Kennedy, and Robert Kennedy.

Back in the day black congregations were very interested in the early Civil Rights Movement so campaigns began at some churches. In fact. I recall several Governors, Mayors and other political leaders attending our church worship services on a regular basis. One well-known comedian was a frequent speaker at our church', and would have Sunday dinner with us, as well as our church leaders, deacons and political strategists of the Movement.

My mom was a speechwriter for many of those leaders back then. It was during that time that I met the late Dr. Martin Luther King. I was five or six years old and my mom told me to come with her to a special choir meeting. I loved to go and hear the beautiful singing, plus she wanted me to learn new songs to accompany her solos. The Pastor called on her to sing for special occasions at the church which made for competition among the ladies. Anyhow. when we arrived at the church, there were many black limousines parked in front, and as we went in, we were searched with a metal detector. I was the only child there and didn't understand what was going on. Mom took my hand, and we went into the choir room. Soon the deacons came in, followed by our Pastor.

The Pastor stood before us and introduced our special guests. I remembered hearing him announce several well known dignitaries. Then he introduced Dr. Martin Luther King, and he entered the room. As Dr. King passed, he shook several peoples hands. When he stopped and reached out his hand, I smiled. He asked, "whose pretty little girl are you?" Mom shyly said. "mine." I remembered he spoke kindly but definitively. He spoke of turning our nation around through non-violent protests. "Resisting the status quo," as it is related to race relationships. I listened intently. Those who came with him had varying opinions about protesting without guns or violence. They said we needed to "fight fire with fire." Dr. King brought up how Ghandi changed India without using weapons, but through resistance. I agreed with Dr. King, who also brought up Jesus Christ as the great reformer of history. It was pretty late in the evening when the meeting ended. I asked mom why the people who came with Dr. King seemed to have different views than the things he spoke about, and she said, "I don't know." I left the question alone.

When Dr.King was assassinated a few years later, I wondered about that night. Later as minister, in church I learned that sometimes people are with you just not always in agreement with you.

The day John F. Kennedy died was a sad day for Americans and the World. It seemed that many people of all races loved all the Kennedys. John represented hope for Civil Rights and equality. The Kennedy's lives were considered magical, an era of Camelot and change. John spoke lofty ideas of an America in which we as free people could transform ourselves from the inside out, where "peace could have a chance, and people made love, not war."

Things were changing; youth were questioning the wisdom of traditional thinking and people were questioning whether we should fight wars to establish free democracies. Race relations were at the center of many controversies in America.

I had met the Kenney's while attending morning worship at our local church. Any political social, or cultural changes that took place during the '1960's involved the churches of the time.

Politicians seemed to rely on godly people to lead the charge and churches relied on legislations made by Politicians to move forward towards changes. The Kennedy brothers had spoken from our pulpits at least twice, that I remember. I also remember a time when we drove my sister to Lake Geneva, to perform opera for the leader. I was fond of our church and family's involvement in the struggle for equality. We lead the weekly rallies as a family, in the Civil Rights protest marches for years, my mom even wrote keynote speeches for prominent spokespersons at the rallies. I believed that her involvement was behind the racial changes taking place in our state.

Even while it was slow, steady, progress is still progress. Then the fateful day came that seemed to crush our collective dreams. It was a normal school day, at least it started out to be. My teacher sometimes got headaches, and would send me to the drugstore across from the school, to pick up some bromo quinine. She asked me to go during recess. As I headed back across the street, I saw a flash in my mind, and then I saw President Kennedy shot, in a convertible! I was shaken! I handed the pills to her, then ran down the block, home. I was scared and my heart had a sinking feeling. How could I have seen that? I ran in the house, past dad, and went straight to my bedroom. I knelt down and prayed.

All of a sudden, I heard wailing from every home. My Aunt came rushing into our living room, screaming, "Turn on the Television!" Then my other sisters and brothers ran in, shouting hysterically! People were falling on the ground.

Lunchtime was over and we hurried back to school, where our teachers could barely hold it together. I kept quiet never saying what I knew, until this writing. I realized later that I only saw that happen; I didn't cause it to happen. Still it troubled me.

Mayor Andrew Young (D-Atla

Chapter 7

GOD'S DIVINE HAND AND PROVISION IN MY LIFE

My life has been ordered by the Word of God. I believe He was very specific in saying what He was going to do in my life. Psalm 23, Psalm 24, Psalm 18, Isaiah 54,Isaiah 55, Isaiah 60, Isaiah 62, Psalm 89, Psalm 93, John 1, John 17, John 14, John 15, Romans 8, Romans 12, Hebrews 11, Rev. 3, Rev 21.

As a child, I had favor with teachers, law makers, community advocates and dignitaries. Though young and untrained I had a "knowing" about things that we'd call political. I believe it was I would tag along with my mom to a lot of important meetings with leaders, pastors and decision makers I picked up valuable tools.

Here's the thing mom knew about me that few in our family understood.

I was like a sponge when it came to remembering what people said and did. I could remember how a song was played on the piano months after hearing it. I could recite speeches that I heard exactly as I heard it. This ability was heightened when it came to dance and singing. Mom knew I could do this and would send me along with my sister to her ballet, piano, and accordion lessons because lessons were expensive and I didn't ask to take the lessons. I was young and quiet so professors, as they were called, didn't mind me being there. But because of "sponginess," they were giving me "free" lessons. We'd come home and I was excited to practise all I had learned at ballet, piano, and accordion lessons.

One day after accordion lessons my sister was outside playing baseball with our neighbors. I thought it was a perfect time to practise what I had stored up in my memory from those accordion lessons. I played for hours until I had perfected the polkas I heard. My mom was in the kitchen and yelled upstairs to where that festive music was coming from, "You are improving with that accordion!" My sister yelled back to her, I'm not playing, I'm outside!

Mom was shocked to find out not only could I play the accordion, but later when the Lawrence Welk television Show came on, I could play the songs they featured on piano. This would serve me well. When I worked at the Jail, as a Chaplain, a minister from South America invited our family to a Christmas dinner. After we ate, all of us gathered around the piano and sang caroles. He had an accordion and I accompanied our singing. It was a very special night.

I also tagged along to many of my sister's ballet classes. I would just sit there, watching and listening to the professor. Again, after we came home, I practised all I had seen only I followed the teacher's movements, instead of the students. Oftentimes, I went along and watched the teacher, who was a fine talented dance instructor and I mimicked his every step. I felt dance was another natural talent given to me, and found myself dancing like Shirley Temple, Bo Jangles, Ginger Rogers and others. I even perfected the ability to do Latin dances like the Flamenco.

Mom recognized my forte for dance and got me booked to perform at several local venues. I was having fun discovering the many things I could do.

As I grew more confident, my mom began to bring me challenges. Once she realized my memory capacity, she read to me "The Gettysburg Address," which I performed for about three years when I was five to eight years old. Then she taught me "Twas the Night before

Christmas," which I performed each year at somebody's Christmas program. Anyway, I was having fun.

I had a wonderful Godmother named, Cecila Ambrose, a close friend of my mom, who lavished me with beautiful dresses, hats, dolls, and jewelry. I loved her smile and she always said she was Glad. I was her "namesake." She attended everyone of my performances and seemed to cry every time I did well. God will send people to bless you.

This beautiful lady would see that all our Christmas' were bright and would load our tree down with presents. One year she had her brother dress as Santa and deliver all sorts of gifts and goodies. Thank you Celia! This went on for years until I turned 11. I didn't know what happened. She stopped coming around. My singing had also developed so that I could sing anything I heard. I still enjoyed performing.

God provides. Growing up with twelve kids (8 biological and 4 adopted), in a household has challenges, from fourteen pairs of shoes when you include my parents, fourteen mouths to feed, at least three times a day. Endless school supplies were needed, and mom was very good at making ends meet. There was nothing ever wasted and everything had its place. Our house was well-kept and with so much going on we had lots of rules to follow. Dad governed everything outside the house, while mom managed our day to day affairs with the house. We had menus that were planned a week in advance and we were expected to do chores regularly. Our house was big, as was our yard. I remembered counting the twenty four windows that had to be washed, six big bedrooms, kitchen, dining room, three baths, and a full basement. Every child older than six had assigned chores and we got them done or else. Or else? You just got them done, that's all. We did have nannies at times too. My mom worked as a medical secretary and a tax accountant in the evenings, so we had nannies during the day. I remembered one, she didn't say much but you always knew what she meant. She was an older woman, Mother

Ferguson, who wore a gray uniform, hat, and orthopedic shoes. She ate figs everyday, and made me eat one once. She was pleasant and very efficient. Mom could count on her to keep things going just the way she wanted them. When we were all in school, mom felt we didn't need the nannies. It was around this time Aunt Annie and Uncle Roy came to live with us. They were senior Ministers who never had children of their own. They had adopted a child that was in the military, so mom took them in. Money began to be tight and I found myself having to get new things more and more. Mom worked hard and dad took on a lot of repair work in our neighborhood. I couldn't complain. Once I needed shoes since mine were worn out. I mentioned it to mom and she said, "we will see." That meant I was at the bottom of the list. A month went by and no shoes. I had a thought. "Somehow I'm gonna get some shoes," kind of like a wish. I wasn't sure if it was a prayer or not. I just kept saying to myself, "I'm gonna get some shoes. "In my heart I believed I was to have new shoes.

Then one day my brother and I were walking to school, I looked down, and saw a Ten dollar bill folded up, right in front of me! I picked it up, and started dancing about, screaming, "My shoes, my shoes, my shoes!"

Afterschool, I couldn't wait to tell mom what I found. I know now that God had provided for my need. Mom took me right away to buy a new pair! Woohoo! Several miracles of divine provision took place in my young life, including winning a paid four year scholarship to a private High School.

CHAPTER 8

GOD'S FAVOR OPENS DOORS AND MIRACLES

God's favor surrounds me like a shield. I would not audition for a particular role but directors would choose me for the lead role, sometimes offending the person that auditioned for it. Once I was on tour with a theater company, performing the role of a mom. The tour was sponsored by the Theatre Board of Directors, who decided how long the tour would continue.

One of the Directors nudged me and asked why I was not in the lead role? I whispered "I didn't audition for it," but he said "We can't keep our eyes off of you!" Later our director announced that there was going to be a change in roles, that I had to learn to entire script and leading role, within 24 hours.

This sort of favor happened to me all the time. In grade school I was selected for the all-city instrumental concert, but didn't audition. In High School I was selected President of Glee Club (there were only six blacks in the entire school, and I was Vice President of the French Club. I was a transfer student to Southern Illinois University.

I was registered as an independent student, meaning I received less than 50% percent of my financial support from my parents. The College I transferred from was closing due to funding issues. I had been accepted at the University, and everything was in place financially. I was to receive an academic scholarship, housing, books etc., through a Pell grant.

I went to collect my financial aid package was told I had no finances available due to an IRS error. After I spoke to mom, she realized her mistake and immediately filed a revision. I was told that change might take up to a month and classes would begin one week away. I prayed and just knew God hadn't brought me all that way to leave me. Amen.

While at the financial aid office I met a guy who asked me if I would come to a college church he attended, if I was still there on Sunday. I agreed. That was Wednesday. Each day I attended my classes even though I wasn't listed on the teacher's roster. After class I went to the financial aid office to see if there was any other aid available. One of my professors noted I never raised my hand at roll call and said starting Monday, every student had to be on his roster to attend class. Then I panicked. God help me, I cried. The financial aid office had no new updates. I was frozen. Tears flowed from my eyes. I thought and I thought. Then a single thought changed everything. That Sunday morning I had attended the church suggested to me. I didn't see the guy that invited me, but the Pastor introduced someone who might know how to help. He was university's President. I headed over to his office. I was told he was across Campus but should return in an hour. A little disappointed, I turned and sniffled. The kind secretary said, "But you can wait if you'd like." She then offered me a cup of coffee. When the President walked in, his secretary whispered, "She's been here for an hour." He turned and headed directly to and whispered, "How can I help you Miss?" I burst into tears!! He took my hand and said, "hold my calls," to the secretary. He led me into his office, grabbed a box of tissue, handed me some and waited until I could speak.

He listened intently. Then he asked what is the grade point average that I transferred with. I told him 3.7. He went to his desk. Turning to me he said, "You were at the Rockhill Baptist Church Sunday?" I shook my head. He called his secretary on the intercom told her to get Dean of Students, Financial Aid Department Head, The Bookstore Manager and my Housing Manager on a conference call and didn't care if they were at home!

I thanked him and Jesus! The university President told them that he wanted me registered and classes, with books and supplies, He promised the Housing Manager he would personally see that my rent was taken care of. He asked them to come to his office and meet his new friend. They did! And he introduced them to as my new family! These people came to performances I was in throughout my next four college years! Talk about Favor!

My Sophomore year in College brought incredible experiences in my faith development and in relationships. I had met a wonderful guy my first year who had asked me to marry him while we were on summer break. I was excited and there was also some concern. I met a guy, who was from Iowa, which never concerned me, up to that point. I had dated several nice white guys over the years but he wanted to wed me. I told him I would give him my answer in the fall when I returned to campus.

Over the summer I turned my life over to Christ and was totally changed. I began to question everything, including my future with him. I was knew in my faith so I relied on my elders for advice. They said I shouldn't marry unless the guy was also in Christ. I was convinced that my friend needed to be saved and was excited to tell him about Christ. He wasn't ready for the life change.

After several attempts I decided to let him go. Six months passed then my friend called me and invited me to a Labor Day picnic with he and his friends. Mistakenly, I thought God was giving me another witnessing opportunity.

We were at Devils Kitchen Lake and he was a wonderful diver off the tall cliff. We were in the Lake til dark. All of a sudden, a huge tree branch punctured the water raft I was on, and down I went. An undertow swept him and I apart. I surfaced three times then settled on the bottom of the deep dark Lake. I must have been down there for at least thirty minutes. Water was pouring into me, and I couldn't stop it. My mind ran to my dear friend, and I pleaded with God to save him because I wanted more than anything for him to be saved. Immediately I heard an angelic choir singing every song I ever heard, all at once. I saw a vision of a police officer at the door of my house. I got a tickle in my throat; which made me think I must be drowning. I made peace with God, and heard myself say," I'm ready."

In an Instant, I was being pulled into a boat by a man, a boy with a flashlight, and my friend. There was a "high" that I never felt before that came over me. When we got to shore nobody said anything. Then my friend said, "it was as if you were dead, but now are alive," as I departed the boat. They stared at me as if I was a ghost. At the emergency room, I threw up a few ounces of water, but the doctor said I could go home.

About a year later I was working in a local restaurant, when my friend and his wife were sitting in my section. He explained to me how that near drowning experience brought him face to face with his own immortality. He and his wife had gotten saved, and wanted to come to my church to give that testimony. Praise God! They came the next day and shared it at my church. Praise God.

One day while in college, I fell into a deep sleep. In a dream I saw a beautiful baby girl. She was perfect and had rosy cheeks, big brown eyes, and a smile on her face.

When I awakened I asked the Lord, "Whose cute little baby that was?" " Yours," He said. I chuckled and went to class. This was 1973 when I had the dream.

In 1992, I was married and pregnant with a baby girl. One day God said to me, "Describe her." My mind went back to the baby I had dreamt about, so I described her the way I recalled her. July 26, 1993, I had a beautiful baby girl we named her Blessing. Amen.

CHAPTER 9

A NEW BEGINNING ROOTED IN MY PAST

My love my life. As long as I can remember I been in love with life and love. I was born with a zest for life in all its forms, love of arts, talents, beauty, nature, science, religion, language, and people. I have been in love with God, His creation, and the majestic ways God reveals Himself in it. God is love in everything we see, and know, and understand. It is exquisite and profound in its simplicity. I sense His nearness expressed in people. I didn't comprehend it but embraced the fact that His love existed all around my world.

I saw it in the trees, the wind, storms, a beautiful sky, a sunny day, in a baby's smile, in the sigh of an old man resting, in the excitement of a pregnant woman, in the athlete who ran the best race, and I saw it in me, when God joined me with the man I call "The Love of my life," sixteen glorious years ago, and still do.

God had purposed this man for me before the foundation of the World, and I am forever grateful. He carefully and intentionally prepared every detail of our adventure together so that all either of us could say is, "That was God."

Here's what I understand.

I met a man while I was dating another man, at the Summerfest. I was at the Summerfest with my friends every year. My male friend went and asked a young lady to dance, leaving me standing there. I didn't know dating rules but a good looking "man" saw it and asked me to dance, so I did.

I felt something I never felt before as he took me in his arms. I felt safe and a warmth like a blanket of love caressed me. I remembered thinking, "Oh I sure hope this guy asks me to dance again." As soon as the music stopped, my friend whisked me away saying, "We're leaving!" I never saw that "man" again until 2001. Several years passed and I had gotten saved, gone to Seminary, and was a single Chaplain at the Jail. The irony at the time, was I started to work the day before the 2001 World Trade Center attack on September 10, 2001.

I was to begin teaching Anger Management, Violence Prevention, Bible Study, Ladies Computer Basics, and Intro. To Poetry Classes. Due to attack, the Jail was on lockdown and all classes were cancelled. I had arrived at the Jail already and me and two other full-time Chaplains were ministered to Jail staff who needed comfort and counseling. September 12, my classes resumed. In a dream, God showed me that I was to make sure to give a Bible into any inmate that requested one. I began taking a cart full of Bibles anywhere I travelled in the Jail, kind of as an advertisement. In my classes I told the attendees to let me know if they had podmates that wanted a Bible or other faith-based reading material. We had access to Christian Publishers that donated thousands of Bibles etc., to the Jail, God caused my efforts to succeed and within a year, every inmate that wanted a Bible had one. I began every class with prayer shared the love of Jesus every chance I could. Soon those attended my classes started witnessing throughout the Jail. I asked the director of our Program whether we could Christen those who professed Christ, repenting of their sins and he said we could. So we Christened 20 inmates each week, giving certificates of baptism to each of them.

While working there I also met a man, with whom I had opportunity to have many conversations with. We talked of my idea to have my students write poetry as an outlet. This gentleman that I met also wanted to try his hand at writing poems. My staff had typed the rough drafts of the writings. She commented on one poem entitled, "Masterpiece." She typed it and handed it to me, to read. I was floored by the genius of it, and the clear pictures given. I was immediately jealous of this object of such brilliance! I was offended. I felt myself turning "green," as I read it. I made a point to find out the "muse" that inspired such a masterful poem. The Man apologized for causing my distress. The next day he wrote another poem entitled, "Beauty You Never Forget." This time my boss told me, "I think he likes you." My secretary agreed. I wasn't interested in him like that. It seemed like a joke and I told my secretary there's no way I could be interested in him, a guy with a recent ex-wife. I didn't matter that he was divorced since I said I wouldn't be interested in a man like him. Then a strange thing happened to me.

I was scheduled to preach at a Chicago church, in my professor's stead, in about two weeks. I was looking forward to the opportunity with great anticipation. When I got home from work after saying, I wasn't interested in the man who wrote incredible poems, I couldn't speak at all. I could barely whisper. I didn't have a cold. I used lozenges, nothing helped. For one week and a half, I had neither a speaking or singing voice. I was praying and fasting. Two days before I was to guest preach, I asked God to reveal the "hidden" to me. In my silence, a small voice began to remind me of what I had spoken to my secretary. Over and over it prayed. I didn't understand still and asked God for clarity. He said, "Zacharias and John the Baptist." I got my Bible out and read the account how the Lord made Zacharias be silent so he wouldn't speak against what God was doing in their lives. I realized that God was doing a new thing in our lives. I immediately repented of my arrogance. The Lord forgave me and had me call my secretary to ask her to forgive my arrogance because God can do anything but fail. And if God was joining me to this amazing man, I would not speak against it ever again. I was able to preach mightily on Sunday. The next week Jeff called me and asked me to marry him. On our wedding night Jeff revealed that it was him that asked me to dance, at Summerfest back in 1972! Neither of us knew each other's name, it was something God revealed to him the day Jeff saw me while I toured the Jail. It never ceases to amaze me how God's plans unfold. Praised The Lord!

God's providence and relationships. I always believed in the beauty of love, and the sanctity of marriage. It was something I desired from an early age. After all, I grew up in the 50's and 60's where families were presented everywhere as functional not fictional. A dad, a mom, and at least two kids, a dog and good neighbors. I saw that beautiful pattern all over television and in my own neighborhood. My mom was the main cook in our household, but dad could make the best buttery biscuits, sugar cookies, and even ice cream. Mom always was clean and dressed to be seen. She wore beautiful pearls and aprons of lace, never walking around in bed cloves or hair rollers in her hair. No she was the example of a good wife that loved her husband and was always making it better. I never saw my mom in slippers, no, she always wore pumps or high heels, for special occasions. Her hair was always neatly coifed her lipstick perfect. I knew she and dad had something special the way they looked at each other and the way they talked to each other. I watched them as if I was watching a great love story on television. The way my mom grew shy when dad complemented her on her hair, or when dad talked about fixing something mom would say things that made dad sit up a little bit in his chair. Once I watched from my upstairs window, my dad working under our car. It was super hot that day. I saw mom walking down the sidewalk, a kind of saunter towards him carrying a clear glass pitcher and a glass of lemonade with ice. Though I never heard either of them speak I watched mom hand dad that cold drink. She stood there as he quenched his thirst and poured him another. Dad pulled out his clean handkerchief and wiped his brow. He quietly kissed mom on the cheek and she turned and slowly sauntered towards the kitchen door. Dad stood there and watched her beautiful self go out of his sight with a smile on his face. That day I knew I wanted That! I wasn't sure of what it was but it gave me a good feeling inside. I knew mom as a woman had something I wanted. She never doubted herself or how she looked. She was very feminine. She did what she wanted to do. She used to make our clothes, beautiful clothes because she could. Mom made special days spectacular days and she enjoyed them as much as we did. She cared for others too. We opened our home to strangers who needed help. We were always bringing some "stray" home for mom to take care of and she did. She would feed them, give a bath and change of clothing. She'd sit them down after dinner and find out how she could help. In the morning she would take them to an agency with resources. Growing up I thought we were rich, but we weren't. Mom and dad were always helping people and taught us that we could always do something to help someone in need. That God made us to make our world better. I have to admit it. As kids I didn't always get that. Sometimes I felt we had less than I wanted when others had nothing and that my mom's love was being used on my adopted cousins, or neighbors instead of me. I know. Selfish right? But when my mom took in our senior Aunt and Uncle to live with us, I understood better. Aunt Annie and Uncle Roy were at one time well-to-do preachers but had no children. Uncle Roy was from Canada and Aunt Annie was from Indiana. They later adopted our cousin, Henrietta. She had grown up and went into the military, so mom moved the couple to our house. I remembered them from when they would visit often when they were younger, always bringing gifts to us kids. Aunt Annie always wore luxurious furs and lovely jewelry and Uncle Roy wore top hats. Now they were feeble and needed help with dressing and bathing etc. Mom in her wisdom gave me the assignment of taking care of the pair while mom went to work. Scared as ever is what I felt. I prepared breakfast and lunch for them. I did the best I could without any training. I learned a lot about myself too. I learned patience and to secure places in our home before putting them in it. I learned to read nonverbal signals. I never asked my mom why she gave me that assignment since I was a middle child of eight and had three older sisters. Now II realize it was a part of God's life training for me. Then when my dad's brother got sick and couldn't take care of himself we also moved him to our home. Uncle Knowledge stayed with us until he passed. Again, I was assigned to be caregiver. My dad also helped a lot because of his brother's size. I believe my mom chose me cause I loved taking care of babies when I was younger, helping mom out with my two youngest brothers from birth til school age. At least that's what I told myself. I didn't understand many of the things I was called to do but somehow rose to the occasion. In college I needed to supplement from student assistance by working. I lived near a Nursing Home. It had a training program so I began there. The experiences I had gotten taking care of senior citizens in pud family, served me well as a CNA. I really liked working there and learned a lot about aging people. I prayed that God would not let anyone die on me too. I thought that would make me want to quit and I needed the job. I worked 11pm to 7am daily. That was fine cause I could take classes during the day and work at night. I worked there three years then volunteered as a church minister later. I never knew I would that sort of care too one day. Thank you Jesus.

MASTERPIECE

As she walks
She seems to glide
As if suspended on air

When she smiles
A brightness emanates
And it shines most everywhere

When she speaks
You hear a songbird
And your heart races

When she arrives
She brings to all
Huge smile on their faces

If you only see her briefly
You still sense her inner peace
More precious than a Rembrandt
This exquisite masterpiece

When she laughs
It sounds like music
So pleasant to be heard

When she's silent
I find myself
Just longing for her words

In her eyes
You see a wisdom
And a depth that pulls you in

When she waves
Even the toughest
Display a silly grin

A vision of enchantment
May wonders never cease
Monet would be enamored with
This gorgeous masterpiece

As she moves
She is so graceful
You feel inadequate

As she draws near
Her scent will linger
So that you can't forget

If she's nearby
The air electrifies
Composing her a song

When she withdraws
I'm blessed with memory
So her images carries on

An aura so radiant
It soothes the savage beast
A face to move Michelangelo
A God given masterpiece

May Whomever has her heart
Make her his queen at least
And never take for granted
This raven haired masterpiece

BEAUTY YOU NEVER FORGET

Sunset near the lakefront
On one of many unremarkable days
My attention focused on a vision
That thoroughly captured my gaze

My eyes caught an image of loveliness
Effortlessly gliding my way
Time seemed to stand still in an instant
As I searched for words to say

A Venus with skin of hazel
Who moved like a leopard uncaged
Her hair skimmered like satin
Then briefly our eyes engaged

Her eyes were dep pools of ebony
Exciting, and yet so serene
Her skin appeared so silky smooth
No greater beauty have I ever seen

What creature could disarm me so
And still we have not met?
I knew then I had encountered
Beauty that you never forget

Her body seemed lithe and supple
And she exuded no hostility
My blood seethed as she came closer
Without a word she had captured me

As my eyes consumed her completely
My mouth dried; my tongue seemed so thick
I must at least say something
To one so very exotic

Closer, I noticed her full lush lips
They would make any man want to kiss her
I needed to say a firm hello
But my voice came out in a whisper

What woman could unravel me so
And capture me in her net?
My mind completely inundated
With beauty that you never forget

I don't know if she heard my greeting
But my eyes spoke volumes you see
With a wink and a saucy flick of her hair
She smile and said "hello" to me

As she sauntered by me quickly
The scent of jasmine enveloped my brain
In an awkwardness I had missed my chance
At this beauty to attain

She left me with no thoughts of sex
I felt only tranquility
Daily men must supplicate for her favor
Even her rejection could be sweet

And still I rave until this day
Of the way that my heart leapt
As I remember the twenty seconds of a lifetime
And the beauty I'll never forget

CHAPTER 10

MY OBEDIENCE

Hair has always been important in our family. My mom's family were part Cherokee Indian and African-American. What this means is we have a lot of hair, and most of us have long, strong hair. In our family there were five girls, four with manageable hair and me who had reddish nappy, thick long hair. I also had a sister whose hair was what we termed "good hair."

Good hair meant it didn't need to be straightened by a hot comb to look nice. There were two things that most African-Americans divide you by, the color of brown skin you had, and the texture of hair you had mattered, at least it seemed to in my mind, as I was growing up.

My own hair was really, really coarse and difficult to comb, so I was in pain from age one to about seven; then my mom discovered a hair relaxer. It apparently did not have a patent yet but mom was trying to help me deal with my unruly hair. In fact the product removed all the hair around my hairline, Mom sued the company and took me to a skin specialist for six months radiation therapy and vitamins grew it back. I didn't care about the hair loss because I could finally have a style that looked better.

So, through the years, my hair grew both long and thick. It had become my pride and joy. I was an associate minister at a community church, when it was facing some ethical problems issues. My family and I were committed to prayer and very active in several ministries within the church and community. One evening God informed me that He was going to use me in a prophetic way. He said in preparation for His move I was to cut my long luscious hair off to one inch. After praying to make sure I was in agreement with God on the matter, I cut my long hair. I had never had short hair before. I never liked short hair and didn't want to cut my hair, but I obeyed the leading of the Lord. He used me to speak to the church that was suffering because of offences against the written Word and will of God. Later God began a new work at the church. I give Him thanks and praise for loving His people, the Church.

Chapter 11

BEING KNOWN IN HEAVEN

Making Godly choices brings glory to God. God gives us opportunities to make Him known on the Earth and when we do He is lifted upon the Earth. Earth is ready to see God manifest in someone's life. One of the choices that I made to exalt God above my own personal success came when I was selected to represent black fashion designers worldwide in 1986. I was modeling for a Fashion Magazine and Modeling Agency.

My agent met with me and several models letting us know the new project was under way to find a spokesmodel to represent all designers who market black fashion designs worldwide. We knew it to be a big opportunity for the person selected. The process involved Runway, Television, Radio, and Magazine representation. It involved International travel as well. I was honored to be a participant in the early selection process. My Agent didn't care which of us was chosen however, she had gotten word that I was being closely considered. Step 2 in the process was Runway Modeling. Three was a Screen Test before the Worldwide judges. Then the impromptu interviews. It reminded me a bit like a Pageant without swimsuits or the Talent part.

I recall it was a month long series of things we were asked to do, then they took a month or two to look at all the materials they had on all participants.

During the month they were making their decision, I flew home to my town, for a volunteer opportunity to teach a Vacation Bible School, at my home Church. I was to co-teach with my former elementary school teacher. I was thrilled to share Christ with her and the students. The theme was the "Parable of the Seeds!"

You know how VBS works. Four days of taking apart Scripture,then presenting what you learned on the last day before the congregation. My mom let me use her sewing machine to make costumes. In two days we had a play in one Act done. I couldn't wait to present the Gospel to the parents, children and my former teacher.

I received the call from my Agent that I had been selected by the worldwide designers, who wanted to release to the Press. I was happy but not as happy to leave before my One Act play was presented. I prayed about it. What a blessing to be chosen and have my face all over the world! I told my Agent I would come back on Monday. All week I had planned how I would witness to this precious nun, who had been blind to the Gospel since her youth, and her decision to become a follower of Jesus Christ hounded me.

The Friday after the play presentation I got my chance. I explained why we need to be doers not just hearers of the Word of God. She agreed with me but couldn't accept the doctrine of everybody being a sinner, and what I had shared with was a stumbling block to her faith. I realized that the Word of God conflicted with her years of training. She appreciated my efforts but she refused to accept Jesus alone as her Savior. I ended up missing several flights back til I realized God had a different plans for my life at that point. God promised me my personal sacrifice wouldn't go unrewarded. Then there was the time I had been invited to sing at the Reagan Christmas dinner, but had promised my son we would spend Christmas together. I kept that promise too. Again, God told me I had a reward coming. How many of you know God is faithful? My faithfulness to the Lord had been tested over the years many times. Glory to God.

CHAPTER 12

FASTING

Fasting had been a part of my Christian discipline from the beginning. I read how Jesus began his earthly ministry by fasting "40 days." I learned to be a follower of Christ to deny my fleshly desires and seek that which pleases Our Heavenly Father. I started off slowly. I would pray about it and ask God to reveal anything that He wanted me to fast about. At first the Lord was doing a cleansing work in me which often required fasting along with pray and praise. Then God began to teach me about intercession, reaching heaven for others. Often God would have me fast about difficult issues, health concerns or spiritual problems.

Fasting seemed to bring clear focus and miraculous things took place as a result of fasting and prayer. One year God lead me pray for our leaders, fasting meat. Another time it was fasting sweets for two years. Every January I would begin the year with a thirty-one day fast. Often I was led to do a three day fast. I believe fasting helps my focus on the things God wants to take place on earth, and teaches me to trust God more.

Every victory I have had in my Christian life involved pray, praise, and fasting. My life currently is preserved by God's nurturing hand and love for me. God has called me to fast from television, sleep, and things that distract me from kingdom matters. God first is my life's goal.

Chapter 13

ANGELS WATCHING OVER ME

Angelic visitations. Most people believe in angels. They see angels involved in our everyday lives. We about Angels "watching" over us or "bringing us Good News. I have no doubt that Angels are on assignment in my life and countless lives of other earthlings. God use of Angels in significant ways in my own life has made me more sure than ever of His Divine Presence, Power, and Love. My first encounter with holy angels occurred when I was young. They watched over me, protected me once when a baseball hit my eye and knocked it out of the socket. Mom put ice on it and that was it. It went back in place. Another time my brother's neck got punctured through as he fell off onto our broken metal chair spikes. Again it completely healed. Later in life I was coming home late one icy night when my car swerved out of control on top a bridge over the Henderson River. It was spinning then stopped horizontally across the highway. I looked up to see an 18 wheeler speeding toward me as if to T-bone my passenger side front window. I yelled "Jesus, Jesus!" I could see the guardrail in front of me car, but sat in awe as the 18-Wheeler passed right in front of me! On another occasion, Angels were present to protect my unborn son, when my water broke at 20 weeks gestation.

I dropped my ex-husband off at his job at work, and stopped at the grocers for milk. All of a sudden, I felt warm liquid rush down my pant leg. I called him and told him what had happened. I picked him up and we went to the Hospital. It was scary but three doves came and sat on the outside windowsill, bringing peace and calm while we waited for a transport to another Hospital that had a Neonatal ICU. When we arrived three doves again welcomed us and the baby stayed in the womb 12 more days, without a single labor pain. In fact, the doctors were amazed that the water kept replenishing itself til I went into actual labor. The baby was born weighing 1lb.15 oz., at six months gestation. My son, my preemie, turned 25 years old in October, 2019! Hallelujah!

Many times my angels have opened doors, closed others etc., as God has and for that I am eternally grateful.

CHAPTER 14

FAITH MUST BE TESTED

Trials of life made me an intercessor for the kingdom of Heaven. God showed me things in the Spirit that couldn't be known except by Him, often for my own protection and safety. My Senior year in college I was chosen to tour with a Theater group to eight cities, performing evenings and doing acting workshops during the afternoons. The last leg of the tour was a performance at a Hotel in, Chicago. My sister had planned a trip to New York, as a graduation present for me, and we were to fly from Chicago to New York, following my final performance. Mom drove my sister to that theatre production as this was mom's initial attendance to any of my performances. They really enjoyed my performance as did the other audience members. After saying our good-byes to mom, we caught our flight to the Big Apple. Near landing we were informed that the plane needed to ascend 2000 feet due to a threatening tornado, in the atmosphere. Then we heard it had touched down near Manhattan.

It was a little scary but we found ourselves taking cover in the downtown Hotel and out of harm's way. It was at 51st and 8th Street. The next day we found out that neighborhood was called, Hell's Kitchen. Our hotel room had no locks and one common bathroom, so you know we were only safe because of Jesus.

We discovered that God had special reasons for sending us to NY other than to celebrate my graduation. For example, we learned to trust the Lord when we wandered in front of Central Park, late one night and met a very, very drunk, smelly man trying to "talk" to us. We had been praying that God would lead us to win the lost, and clearly this man was lost. He had a boombox blasting music, and we studied how when one person would speak, the other would pray. That method worked sometimes, so we tried that.

Surprisingly the man turned down the boombox. He began to listen, and the next thing I knew, the man was crying loudly right there in front of Central Park! He asked us to pray for him. Then we went deeper and deeper into the Park, when we heard a voice saying, "What you two doing here this late?" It was very dark. We stood still and the voice got closer. We saw it was a policeman, and he said we must be tourists, cause New Yorkers know better. He said he would lead us out of the Park, and we followed him out. He took us out to where we first entered the Park, and we saw that man; we had witnessed to, now preaching to everyone on the street!

The next day we caught a ferry to Liberty, to see the Statue of Liberty. While on the ferry people kept coming up to me, asking questions in Venezuelan, Portuguese, Colombian, Mexican, and Spanish. My sister turned to me and asked," Why are they asking you?" I said, I don't know! When I looked back on that day, I realized something. The folks asking me resembled me. Later, I called my mom and asked if I could possibly be mixed with South American? She said, "Maybe."

I remembered growing up thinking I was some kind mixed person, Italian people were drawn to me, you know our city has a very diverse mix of nationalities there. I know there were Sicilians in my family's ancestry, as well as Africans, and Venezuelans. When I married' I lived in the International Housing section of the university, where I met a lady from that country, and she looked like my mom and me. It would take another six years before God revealed me to me. A friend of mine had invited me to visit a church with her. So we went.

God purposes amazing things for those who love Him. When he brought me to Jeffery, my husband He told us we were going to have a "New Beginning." Everything about our wedding and lives has been ordered by God and we have an awesome life together. Here's what I mean. We prayed and asked God to lead us in every aspect of our bridal plans and He announced to us that He wanted the colors to be white for holiness and red for the Blood of Jesus. He told us He wanted everybody in the bridal party to wear white, including the bride, groom, bridesmaids, groomsmen, flower girl, minister, and Guests. Guests? Yes, God said guests. We were to invite the entire Church and God instructed us on who was to stand up in the bridesmaids and groomsmen and why! Everyone of them was to be married or a widow, or widower, celebate single person, in covenant with Christ. It was a challenge but "obedience is better than sacrifice."

When I first called our church some thought we would have a problem with the everyone dressing in white, due to our wedding being in August. Some felt that most white dresses were worn by only brides and this might limit peoples' choices, but I said, "if God said it He would make it happen."

Money was going to be a challenge, but after private prayer, people began to come to me and volunteer everything from a lady who bought the wedding cake, to people who volunteered to cook a beautiful reception dinner. I realized that when you choose to do things God's way, He will make a way. I had never so much as tried on a wedding dress before, and was concerned about how I would look. I dreamt about me in a beautiful bridal dress but had never actually shopped for one. God lead me and Blessing to go to the Bridal shop. They had unusually beautiful dresses and before I could panic over the prices, a lady came up to me and asked if was there for their once a year bridal fair? I asked what that was. She told me they sold beautiful bridal gowns for $99! She told me where they were. Surprisingly, there was only one dress in my size left on the rack. When I tried it on everyone in the shop gasped for joy! Blessing was so happy too! They had to take it in a little but it was the dress of my dreams! Praise God! Everything God told us He wanted was done and we had a Holy Matrimony! It looked like Heaven at our sunset wedding!!

CHAPTER 15

THE CALL TO SUFFER FOR CHRIST

I never knew there was such horrific pain before this. I imagined that all surgeries involved pain, or that being shot with a gun, probably had a pretty severe level of pain accompanying it. I had a leg amputated and suffered incredible pain. I had heard of people having pain management that included high doses of morphine etc. to silence the feelings of pain, but had no point of reference for the kind of "mind-numbing, inescapable" pain I recently experienced after an amputation. No, I was shocked by the complex suddenness of my inability to avoid this pain that came from merely moving my leg, even an inch. How? Why? What was this about? I prayed. I praised. I pleaded with God. I wrestled with doubt. Finally, I stood on the promises of God, and reminded myself of things that He had said in times past, regarding my life. And I waited. And waited. His sweet Holy Spirit rested upon me. Psalms of affirmation and comfort seemed to wash over me and soon I felt waves of peace carrying away my suffering. My night had become day.

Blessed Savior delivered me once more. "Weeping may endure for a night, but joy cometh in the morning." Hallelujah.

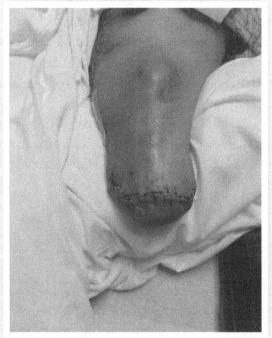

CHAPTER 16

CONCLUSION

God has given me unusual talents to sing anybodies song, whatever I want to sing. I could sing like Barbara Streisand, Whitney Houston, Dionne Warrick, Patti Labelle, Celine Dion, Bette Midler, Lulu, Natalie Cole, Yolanda Adams, Sandy Patti, Tramaine Hawkins, Roberta Flack, Cece Winans, and Anita Baker. I Heard the Lord say that whenever I sang their songs, they would become transformed.

This was particularly true of Whitney Houston. From the first time I heard her record, "You Give Good Love," I knew she and I had similar voices. I sang many of her hits with ease. I began praying for her as I learned her tunes and performed them anywhere I could. Soon God was telling me to pray for Whitney's family. Everytime she did a new album, movie, or was in the news, God had me pray for her. I kept a journal of people God assigned me to, which included, Janet Jackson, Sandi Patti, Michael Jackson, Tina Marie, Regina Bell, Patti LaBelle, Barbra Streisand, Gladys Knight, Yolanda Adams, Anita Baker, and others, who I prayed for daily and sang their songs.

I began to realize this gift when I sang Barbara Mason's "Yes, I'm Ready," back in grade school. All these singers were the one's I admired most when I was young. They helped me to learn breathing techniques, phraseology, pitch etc. I studied their performances til I perfected their songs. Singing, dancing, and Acting had been things I was most regarded for til I met the Lord Jesus. I was excited to sing their songs since they would come to Christ once I sang their hits publicly. Since I met Jesus the Gospel message has been what I am known for, loved for even hated for. All my gifts to perform are tools to share the Gospel. All that I am and all that I have has been utilized to spread this wonderful good news. It is my reason for living. I know that I am in the heart of God, the plan of God and the purpose of God. Jesus is all we need, His Holy Spirit is the most influential tool, given us by God to transform us, and His Grace gives eternal life which is available to everyone. His thoughts concern me and every human that trusts Him.

I share this humble truth because of Jesus, my Lord, my Savior, My Guide, My protector, My Provider and My everything. I am so blessed that I am His and He is Mine. Amen

CPSIA information can be obtained
at www.ICGtesting.com
Printed in the USA
BVHW030953211119
564442BV00006B/63/P